THE BEAUTY

THE BEAUTY OF
THE MOON

Anne Haverty

Chatto & Windus
LONDON

Acknowledgements

Acknowledgements are made to the editors of the publications where some of these poems have already appeared: *Poetry Ireland, The Observer, The Irish Times, Lifelines, The Anglo-Irish Studies Review, Human Rights Have No Borders, The Whoseday Book.*

Published by Chatto & Windus 1999

2 4 6 8 10 9 7 5 3 1

First published in Great Britain in 1999 by
Chatto & Windus
Random House, 20 Vauxhall Bridge Road,
London SW1V 2SA

Random House UK Limited Reg. No. 954009

A CIP catalogue record for this book
is available from the British Library

ISBN 0 7011 6746 7

Typeset by Deltatype Ltd, Birkenhead, Merseyside
Printed and bound in Great Britain by
Creative Print and Design, Ebbw Vale

Contents

For A
again

THE HEAVENLY VIEW OF MANHATTAN

Unseen, like the enigmatic one
Above the clouds, you can
Lie languidly on white sheets and listen
To the roar of Manhattan.

From the thirty-first floor of the Hilton
You can listen to the hysterical flatus of the streets,
Their sullen cabs and shouting crazies,
Loudmouth exchanges, everyday threats,
Distilled to a pleasing and musical hum –
Like the singing of undiscovered birds
Or Cape Cod bees at their sunny and ordered tasks.

To what he, sprawled far, far above on his divan hears,
What he makes of our whimpers and tears.

FROM A TRAIN 1

Two young men in a tilled field
And a horse's ghost with them.

FROM A TRAIN 2

at the close of stubborn light
the secret and obstinate mirror
nested in birches
of an anticipative pond

FROM A TRAIN 3

A long grey house on a hill
Where a woman was sad,
The cooing dove
Competing with the crow,
The windows unpainted.

I will paint them, for
Sadness seeks redemption.
Happiness is a conclusion.

FOR AUNTS

Oh heavenly heart, return
To us our dead aunts.
Give them back to us
In their innocent dresses.
Let us know them
As we know our sisters
And not as women who
Buttered cake for us and kept
From us their secret loves and hates.
Let us write them the letters we did
Not write them on their birthdays
Or on their feast-days in the case
Of those who were nuns.
Let them smile upon us not
With the closed smile of those who know
The disappointments of a woman's life,
Let us want to know what
They wanted to tell us,
Let us go dancing together in the marquees
Where they danced with their charmers.
Oh heart, give them to us
Again to know.

HAYBOY

Hayboy, Hayboy, sun-burned and shy –
'Come in, Jamie, come and have a bite' –
He was working for her all afternoon
and my aunt fussed about his tea.
Fixing his gaze at the tree waving
in the window, Hayboy took gulps
from his cup and bites of ham,
passing me worldlessly the jam
a moment before I was about to ask –
Picked up his cap, and ran.

Next tea-time my auntie fretted –
'Jamie was shy, he didn't eat a bite' –
I saw my place at table was not laid,
his stood alone, his knife and plate.
'Could you sit in the parlour? You won't mind?'
And let him eat in his accustomed peace?'
In purdah on the parlour couch, quiet
as a nun, and chill, I heard him talk
on the quality of hay, the price for barley –
Hayboy, Hayboy, sun-burned and master.

THE FIRST EVENING

Children, like buds, know
When spring has come.
The first evening whose light
Is reluctant to submit and the air's
Rawness is softly cut from the west,
They're out, sprawling alertly
On each other's doorsteps,
New clasps in their hair
And down the corner, lounging
With expectation in pink
And yellow sweatshirts
Humming their urgent songs
As grandmothers make
Their way past to Devotions.
The children in the lane
Who know, like birds,
When spring has come,
Can be, like the singing birds
And the green buds, betrayed.

JACINTA AND THE STONES

Jacinta, usually sad
When she walks by the sea
Lost in thoughts maybe
Of the man or men she walked
With before on other shores
Or of her good young times,
Traverses unseeing the stones
That people the beach,
Alike as men and women are
Though no two the same,
Individual as the uncountables
Who live in the world.

Towards the rusty abandoned Transit
Or some old obsession on her inner
Horizon, she steps, printless but mortal
On their impassive various faces,
Sun-dried, wind-blanched ovals,
Ellipses in forty greens, opals,
Scorched yellows and cassis purples
Heedless, unmarked, unyielding,
Telling her nothing, joy or sorrow,
And careless of her passing.

LINES FROM MALAYA

Aruna Jee Kampong Koh Sitiawan, Perak, Malaysia.
His stamps showed parakeets and jade-green petals.
Warm and damp we turned the palm leaves of his letters
In our school lunchroom by the boiling Burco kettles.

His stamps showed parakeets and jade-green petals.
Scenting odours of rubber, coconut and a man's sweat
In our school lunchroom by the boiling Burco kettles
That winter I wrote a lot to him about our climate.

Scenting odours of rubber, coconut and a man's sweat
I described the look of snow, our temperate ferns . . .
That winter I wrote a lot to him about our climate.
A boy, he wrote of engines in cars and aeroplanes.

I described the look of snow, our temperate ferns . . .
At last I tired; my friend sent word that I was dead.
A boy, he wrote of engines in cars and aeroplanes.
Yes sad, so sad, but might she write to him instead?

At last I tired; my friend sent word that I was dead.
Warm and damp we turned the palm leaves of his letters
Yes sad, so sad, but might she write to him instead?
Aruna Jee Kampong Koh Sitiawan, Perak, Malaysia.

LADIES WAITING ROOM, THURLES STATION

Cool as a milk-churn, bare as a mountain field,
A smoulder of sods in the grate, that winter scent –
Before I came to know her, this room did; the chair,
The butter-coloured walls, the grey wainscotting. Her
Coty powder perfumed its air for an hour –
A voice complains outside; a delay at the Junction –
And Blackie neighs in the station-yard as my ghostly
Grandfather gives him the nod. Now they've gone.

She was a girl in a red coat going back to Dublin.
Some stranger maybe combing her hair half-saw
That precious face in the mirror and remarked
The train was late. My mother, I imagine, agreed;
Politely, absently, as she often did . . . Briefly, I am she.
But what else she said, or really thought, is lost to me.

RIMBAUD

Under your mother's enchantment
In a barbarous village
Your rosy boy's face is going
Colonial red. You are eating
Hashish, Rimbaud, and laying
Up note upon note
Stained with Africa, in a tin

For that province of France
That *beau idéal*,
A paved, low-treed square with
A church, a café, a *pont l'évêque*
Where your future waits.

The haricots are frying
In their yellow paste.
Your *fille* is padding
Round with her foreign
Child inside her.

Go home, Rimbaud, go home.

Come back, Arthur, come back.
We have a plump Alexandrine
For you. Or the thin serious one
With a graceful head whose
Brother you played with in
Compiegne. Remember? He's
A notary now here in
Charleville. The family trade
Goes *pas mal*. But of course
Whichever you prefer.
And don't you worry.
I've made sure of the terms.

For a dealer in timber, Rimbaud,
You have an exotic past.
The rashness of your youth
Has left you in a pit of love
Where the walls bend
Like a grimace before dawn.

To where a mother must not
Die without the sobs of a son in her
Ears, oh return, Arthur, return.

Rimbaud runs like a boy
Desperate at night when the
Country road is mad with ghosts.
Pulled up at Marseilles, his
Emmerdant leg has to come off.
He is too late now, too late.

There is no hope for Monsieur Rimbaud.

In the mild sun of Normandy
A beautiful soldier sleeps
Among the daisies and grass.
In his person, two musket balls
Fresh-stained with red are hiding.

AN ALTERNATIVE LIFE

for the actor who played Tadzio in Death In Venice *and died a drug-related death while still a youth*

Was his father a shipping agent in Stockholm?
Anyway, plucked by Visconti from the gymnasium
He gave a moving and grave performance. Was
happy to do it but remained immune
somehow to the lure of the screen. Read
classics at Stockholm and Oxford, married
his plainer second cousin, works now
in the family business. Goes sailing in the summer
around the fjords, skiing in winter to the Alps, has
developed a surprisingly muscular physique.
Is father of three slim fair-haired children. One
has a short leg − so he's quite prominent
in the foundation for disabled children, accompanies
them on group holidays to Italian resorts.
And yet there's an unlikely expression you can see
At odd moments sometimes, at charity balls. Tadzio's
wistful look, waiting for his real role to begin.

PREPARATIONS FOR THE RECEPTION OF A SOUL

For Swinburne, Symons
Arranged the angels
In rows of three
And organised Goethe
To be there
At the head of
The waiting party.

Bearers of Fernet Branca,
Opium and turkey-legs,
Aids poets use on earth
To attain heaven
He didn't mention.
An expert, he assumed that
After the journey
Poets would live
On the ether of each other.

To welcome in
The ordinary soul
There is the old
Assembly of kith and kin.
An auntie to take your hand,
A long-beloved's smile
To light the path
To the Beatific Familiar.

As usual, I want everything.
Ether and hearth,
Everybody to be there,
Goethe and grandmother,
The young man who
Died in France on the lonely
Rack of the parallel bars

Running with Radiguet
Along our paradise shore.
And the one who is
Locked in my heart.

A perfect university
For the affectionate elect.
A blooming of my first
Stunted year at Trinity,
Uncle floating across the Square
For a word with Mary Anne
Known of course as George
To Browning.

TO A SAINT

We find you much nicer an exemplar than those
old saints you toppled from their plinths
to lie among the nettles in self-mortifications.
Let them mutter that you were one of those schemers,
playing the good people of England against the courtiers,
denouncing the prince, plotting for her son to be king.
They're boring; on endless dry-bread fasts, holy but gaunt –
when renunciation at lunch made you sexy in San Laurent.
You were everyone's ambition, star-struck, wealth-stricken.
As Francis of Assisi fed small birds, you fed the kids
of the paparazzi. And why can't a saint dine at the Ritz?
Especially if she eats salad and then only little bits.

You reached out to us, a lonely princess
Wanting us as you suffered us, in the perfect dress.

DEATH'S GIFT

i.m. Conleth O'Connor

you, whom Fame Eluded, must have heard it often said
by kith and kin mourning your lack of a decent income –
'You could've been rich, with your Brains and Education.
Let's face it. You'll only be celebrated after you're dead.'

early she found you, the pale seducer of your imagination,
dallied in the shades with you, then Took You For Her Own
a joke in the dark, the rank fog on drifting water, your
mutual fascination – such desire she's disinclined to spurn.

now friends are reciting your poems since you are gone, a
modest gathering for a Memorial Reading on a chilly evening,
while outside in the arc-lit square, they're shooting a film
by another writer who is famous, rich, younger, and living.

that Malicious Death has had you every which way seems to be
incontrovertible. Until your words, beautiful and true, hove
into the room. And unmasked, you leap, Noble Poet suddenly,
from the grave. As if, courteously, she pays you for your love.

THE BAG LADIES

From Ballinahinch to
the Eastern Balkans
they talk to themselves in the streets,
they wear a look in the eye
from which everyone turns, it is
the look where the inside and the outside meet.
Now there is frost and they talk of
summers from the past, the roses.
When we are forgetful under the sun, they
talk of winters to come.
They are many
and few of them are loved and
nobody understands them.

AT FONTAINEBLEAU

thinking of my mother

Might she have known joy in the Ile de France,
She to whom God gave too tender a heart,
Have smiled in recognition at a girl-deity's glance?

Following Diana with her hound dogs and her lance,
She who God decreed should ever stand apart,
Might she have known joy in the Ile de France?

In the orange garden where the graven horses prance,
Slighted by those who make that extra effort,
Have smiled in recognition at a girl-deity's glance?

Where the one-armed keeper's peacocks walk in trance,
For her whom God's own doom made gentle as a hart,
Might she have known joy in the Ile de France?

By the winter fountains could she have stood aghast,
Struck by a sun-tipped arrow from a lightning dart,
Have smiled in recognition at a girl-deity's glance?

Too tender ever to join the quotidian dance,
One to whom God gave no consolatory art,
Might she have known joy in the Ile de France,
Have smiled in recognition at a girl-deity's glance?

WHENEVER I THINK OF FRANCIS STUART

Whenever I think of Francis
I think of Easter.
In a warm wind blowing from the west
He is going with his mediaeval monk's
Face to feed a young goat
Leaping on the rock.
Actually it's Autumn and
He's walking in the direction
Of Nassau Street as the
October evening is drawing in,
But it seems the light glows longer
Than it did yesterday and flowers
In the far north that were dying
Out during the afternoon
Are beginning to bloom again.
For the last of the great
Christian festivals left to us
Uncolonised by commerce, we are
Preparing a frugal and sweet repast,
Almonds, chocolate and spring lamb.
Whenever I think of Francis,
Limping like a boy
Who fell out of a tree,
I think of the feast of Resurrection.

THE BIG HOUSE

What will they do without their asparagus?
What will they do without calabrese?
Their summer berries minded from the wasps,
Sweet in constant Mayo rain, in shafts
Of sunlight husbanded by the wall.
The roof is fallen into the hall.
No-one anymore looks in catalogues for seed,
Farther than London they've gone, to oblivion.

Not even ghosts can dine on trees.
The roof is fallen into the hall,
The house gapes like the vacant eyes
Of a gassed soldier in the great war.
Down the basement passage to the stables
Where a lad so lately creaked in silks and leather
To run that race that must be and was won,
Drips echo from cracks in the rent stone.
Cook's warm domain stinks like a dungeon.

Brief as the lilac flowers, delicate
As the young pod of a green pea, the vast
Kitchen garden bloomed before the trees,
Cut down, began to grow again. Bounded by the
Wall, raised brick on tawny brick by souls
Potato-fed for luncheon and for breakfast too
To guard the tender leaf and fruit,
As ascendant forest climbs the sky.
The roof is fallen into the hall.

Luminous, ground ivy under the trees,
The air emerald as phosphorous;
Out of the past, a sun is caught
In the ruddy glow of trunks in gloom;
It's weird and meaningless as a dream.
There is no nut nor bud nor plant,

No hoe nor spade disturbs the earth.
Vendettas always reek of death and
These doomy trees avenge Kilcash.
The roof is fallen into the hall.

SUIT ENVY

He was just a man, no
Taller, darker or handsomer
Than another.

But inside his monotone
Suit that he unbuttoned
With a detached gesture of
Masculine authority, he had
A mysterious breast pocket
With a tenner or two
That he took out to pay
For his beef satay, his
Mr Mash and his diet milk,
Investing our modest female
Task of food-gatherer with
A foreign art and every
Manly virtue, lots of money
At home or in a bank
Somewhere. Control, power,
Necessity implicit in that
Breast pocket reach of his,
Lent even to his shopping list.

In line behind him, I
Wanted, fishing in my purse
And having somehow
Bought too much,
A breast pocket inside a suit,
Seeing what tailors saw
And Freud did not.

MAN TALK

I am growing my hair.
A man never tells a fellow that.
Never says, I bought new shoes,
Brown with laces. Grey always
Suited me. It's my colour.

These are things they decide
About each other in secret,
Slyly observe across talk of
The game, the cabinet changes
And art possibly.

OUR FATHER THE TERRORIST

Father, forgive me.
I cannot of late
but see you as a terrorist.
Seek as I might
to turn my mind
to wholesome thoughts,
still you stalk the dark
plains of the air,
your array of terror
in your belt.

Some you burn,
drown more.
You starve plenty
and infect the hearts
of your children
so that with the daily news
I lose all hope;
and anyway know that
love or hate, we all
will die in the cause
of your obscure ideology,
the pie in your sky
that the cruellest take up
with the most success.

Forgive me Father
if I blaspheme.
This is but the latest
of my sins.

HELLO LEIPZIG 1990

In the late spring we'll go to see you in our shining cars
Cities that have come up from under the sea,
Lvov's stuccoed spires, the faded colours of Budapest
Glistening in our sunlit tourist eyes.
In our cars with foolish or heroic names of racehorses and
Classical girls we are coming to meet you,
Our exotic cousins in the dowdy frocks we admire.
Sowing potatoes in fields dusty with the fall-out of industry
Your faces will grow rosy as we approach,
Your ghostly faces that were receding from us along the
    road east
Of Cracow when we saw you last, to be drowned.
Children of our parents' prodigal hopes, you show us
We are weightless as birds and can float through Warsaw's
    bars.

OMAGH

In town, a transcendent mid-August noon,
Its mood somehow not averagely mundane.

A day condensing a shadowy lost summer,
The toss of shimmery trees already ephemeral.

Intensity of sun, cloud and wind all together,
A day the dead might wistfully remember.

SHE DREAMED OF A WASHING MACHINE

Look at her. A poignant lesson in revolutionary endeavour.
On her old knees in frozen mud on the bank of the river,
A glazed kerchief printing out her cold deaf ears – had a
Fur hat once but Boris took it when he went to Siberia –
In a hole she's made in the ice, rinsing her grandchild's cottons,
Her fingers red as wheaty puddings dyed in cochineal.

And to think she used to dream of a washing machine!
One spring lately, with a dollar she found in the street, she
Bought distemper and washed the common hall in her building
Lettuce green. But it needs a good scrub again –
A bit of soap and a lump of sausage this winter's dream.

At full tilt they passed her by, two revolutions already,
Like bright clouds in an April sky, spattering words,
Their words for her. To her they were all the one master.
The millennium upon her, she's hungrier and colder
And labours more than her own babushka she can vaguely
Remember, who was born in eighteen seventy-four.

CONVERSATION, UNTER DEN LINDEN

They drink? Do they not thirst?

They get no water. None
But what makes up their soup.

Soup? You give them soup?

Of cabbage. Turnip. Made of potatoes
Even a Pole wouldn't eat.

Good. So they hunger a little?

At feeding-times, they get a modest ration
Of the hard grey Galician bread.
I assure you, not much.

They keep clean, I trust?

Washing holds small interest for them.
Naturally. So. When they refuse they do not
Eat. Often we have to whip them in.
Cold water is ample in the showers,
Enough at least to sluice the mud off
And the feeble out. They are pervious
To chills. Pneumonia. The lung.

And love? Tell me something, does
What they know as love survive?

The gaze is vacant. There is nothing
In the eyes. No, they love only to thieve,
One from the other. And lice love them,
To nestle in. You know, Mein Herr, when
They pass me in a herd, tramping stupidly
Through all that Polish muck, their black

Offensive hair shaved off, I see that we
Are creating some new species of brute.

Exactly. We must finish what God began.
And the able. They are working well?

Like oxen. Until they drop. What animal
Will not answer to a blow?

But also dying well I hope?

Indeed. Some hundreds daily. Often
Thousands. Our system is discreet,
Efficient, quiet and cheap. When
Labour is to hand and free, what can
Not be achieved. No mess, no fuss,
Their flaccid bones reduced to
A fine pale calcine powder.

Ah yes. Calcine. What you're here
To discuss. More coffee? Good, isn't it.
Now. To what use could this be put.

HOUSE MOVE

Where we began were enormous trees, shadows and a sun
   so bright –
Now, bending our heads at the swish of a nun's dark habit, we
   weep for the dog that died.
Naked panes blinking at dusk, there were acres of field
   around every house –
The rows of windows in town are blinded or decently
   clothed in lace like altar-boys.

Raspberry groves, giant lupins, someone sent on the bike for
   ice-cream wafers –
Then First Communion and the priest's frown at a girl's
   mispronunciation of pray-for-us.
Gathered in secret places, our first pencils were the purple
   phalli of wild arum –
Here we buy biros and copybooks and parse sentences for
   teacher's approval.
Singing on dandelion roads, our country pals, picturesque
   as Pan in coats too short –
While we are cast among towngirls, artful, fragrantly toxic
   in well-fitting frocks.

All one winter week, the convent looming before us, we
   burrowed inside,
feeding like moles on Beauties of Bath and old books from
   a flotsam of tea-chests.
The boy was enrolled in a class where he would learn to box,
   provision for his self-defence,
and we were led to the dressmaker's to be measured
   for our blazers.

Waking to a world grey and small, the new house on the
   town's bleak edge,
hiding our faces in withered apples and books – That week
   we fell to earth.

MOTHER AND DAUGHTER IN BEWLEY'S CAFE

Farther and farther they go into silence,
Eat their grill and then their gateaux
Knowing how to do this together.

There's something alike.
A look about the mouth that will
Fold with time in the same way,
Hair that may only have faded from
How the younger's is. But really,
You could never tell.

The mother, appalled
At the unfair passage of the years,
Gazes sullen as an adolescent.
In carriers around her feet,
New clothes for winter no-one
Will notice. Except her sister
Who'll ask first how much.

Nothing to say, they nurse
Their secrets. Dreams
Of deceit, of love, of glory.
An unfilial future. A makeshift past.

Idly, Girl spoons the sugar,
Applauds Mother's empty plate
And, splendid eyes downcast, frankly
Unreins her filly's mane for a boy
In the corner bored with his tea.
Mother sees what her mam saw –
No sooner here than gone.

DO

The winding-sheet
That is my life
May now be only
Half-undone.

Days that make
Ghosts of the living,
Turn the wedding-suit
Of the proud groom
Into the comical
Garb of a bent man
Shouldering a rake
In an August field.

Yet I still wait
To tell them
How when his key
Turns in the lock
The world
Enters the room.

And the winding-
Sheet that is my life
Winds tighter
Hour by hour.

END OF THE CENTURY VERSE

Where is the grave?
Not far, not far.

Will she be there?
Who can say? Only she.
And she is not here.

How much time do I have?
Not long, not long.
And all roads lead there.
Whatever turns you make
None of them is wrong.

Dark clouds are climbing briskly
Up the sky. Shall I go
Out tonight? Or wait inside?
In the Prater the twilight lamps
Of cycles open and close among
The trees, weave their covert paths
Beneath the chestnut leaves.
And nothing compares, nothing
Compares to you, sings again
And again an *Irische kind.*

The big wheel is keeling
Over heavy and slow.
Not far, they say, not far.
But how near? How near?

APRIL IN A TEMPERATE CLIME

Cows wear dun coats like their mother's mother,
And the people wear jackets they wore in November.
In five degrees plus or so of chill from the east,
Breaths in clouds disperse before they form; still
Cold enough for hunched backs and steam from a Gaggia
To float in the torpor of the station buffet.
The abolished Limbo has come down out of the skies
To take up its habitation in the space for April,
Heaven has moved far off and Hell is disbanded.
Nothing will die, nothing is born,
The duckweed in the stagnant pond is exhausted.

LLEWELLYN POWYS IN DAVOS

I coughed up blood in my couchette
As we crossed the sunlit fields of France.
I know the colour of that blood,
Thick, arterial, crimson-red.

At last as it was getting dark
Our train ran into Davos Platz.
The porters at the station all had
A hotel or a sanatorium's name
On the brims of their hats.
They brought us up here in sleighs
Past lighted chalets where figures
Lay prostrate on balconies.

My room, number fourteen, is fine.
Number thirteen has been omitted.
This thought obsesses me –
That mine is the one left out.

A doctor examined me in the afternoon.
He assured me I could live a long time.
At dinner I sat at the English table, between
Two young men who have it in their throats.
They do not talk. One is a clerk from Leeds.
They are able to converse by passing notes.

Have I told you about the rich young Russian
Who is in love with a little compatriot? But alas
She loves a Hungarian who's quite emaciated.
What a little barbarian she is, slender and delicate.
The Russian is jocular on the gravity of his illness,
Talks of his weeks on the Steppe drinking koumiss.
I, however, see the death terror in his eyes. Truly,
The cold freshness of the air here is delicious.

Last night, my little barbarian drank too much champagne.
I sat up late with her and the Hungarian.
Your life-line is a good one, I was able to tell him.
'A good one?' He laughed. 'Considering I am dying . . .'
He is devoted to Napoleon and showed me his mementi.
'That is my past,' he said, pointing to his bureau,
'And there my future is.' He gestured towards his bed.

All day the frozen mountains glitter
In the sun, which here is much brighter.
The Russian showers his love with flowers
And brought a band from town to entertain her.
She seems to notice him hardly at all.
They say we are having a fancy-dress ball.

In the night one of the Englishmen
Had a serious haemorrhage.
I heard the nurse emptying the basin
And him asking her if he would live.
Yes, certainly, the doctor said.
But by evening he was dead.

I dressed as an Asian prince in gold and scarlet.
There was a bride, an emperor and a pierrot,
Everyone in such high spirits, champagne, laughter.
Were it not for the coughing, we could have
Made at the ball such a gay and colourful picture.
My little Russe was absent and, going in search of her,
I came upon the servants carrying away a corpse.
Hushed and in stockinged feet, they were
Secretly taking it to the dead-house in Davos.

It is never pleasant for live patients
To meet a dead one coming down the stairs.
Across the white and empty plain, I gaze
At Davos, town of dreadful death, forsaken,
Its black church spire like a devil's finger.

My wild, my little wilful barbarian.
She it was they carried away that evening.
Her Russian shot himself in the chest.
But by an odd irony, his illness has
Moved his heart from its place
And he is pitiful but still with us.

Small flakes of snow were falling at noon.
I was glad to get back to my room again
And drew my curtains once I regained my bed.
I have a touch of fever and some discolouration.
It is certainly a result of this heightened state
But the mountains just now, shadowed by twilight,
Look queer to me, as if streaked with blood.

LAST DAY OF SUMMER

After a yearning month of June
The wasp that buzzed once
Has idled and fallen.
After a blast from the Jokuls
The geranium's brave petals
Are scattered and blown.

The dog renews his frosty bark
Resuming the stony roads
And nursing his paw.
Deauville and Trouville, luminous
For Dufy and his girls' parasols
In the young century, await the
Bleak compensatory light
Of *le mois d'août.*

In the low mute temperature
We cannot heat
We pull our thick jackets of hurt
Close about us and 'Fine,'
We say, wearily, 'Fine,'
It's all over now,
Even the shouting.

HE COMPARES UNIVERSITY COLLEGE DUBLIN
TO THE CHINESE UNIVERSITY OF HONG KONG

Yup. The restaurant has ham with pineapple,
Hi-Energy drinks to overcome the malaise of the suburbs
And their langour under a grey post-colonial sky,
Air dense with the closeness of a dull July.

Two architects maybe had the same idea. Or
One had two the same. A forcing-house for
Eager kids from east or west, raised in pastures
Where cows once munched on scented flowers
Or paddy-fields with buffaloes to pull the plough.

Perfume of poppies and mimosa intimating
Faintly another life, a possible bliss, were bliss
Not bleached by afternoons of monotone-ness,
Trudging up the steps to Civilization,
Around the blocks in their T-shirt uniform.

At least life after might always seem an
Almost-heaven . . . Here, they are well-prepared
For the brutal world, you can at least say that.
And then a national bureau will take them on.

Hi, they say with the greedy cheer of the normal
Ambitious. A wild rose here, honeysuckle there,
Clinched in a concrete kiss, and shrinking
Violets pushed into the even-tempered pond,
In which many a pale lotus has drowned.

IN THE COUNTRY

In the country there are youths
With the sweet breath of sucky calves
And their soft mouths.

WHERE DOES THE MONKEY SLEEP

Where does the monkey lay her head?
Why does memory flap on the wind
And where does the condor build his nest?

Whom do we love? How when we must soon be done
Does our little happiness protect our rest?
Why aren't we made of wood or stone or even bone?

Why are we such a clever breed –
Though we seem stupider than before?
Were they authentic, who were alive some years ago?

Why must we ask and not be told?
And why when fed
Some fragile answer do we then forget?
The truth is always what we cannot know.
How does the monkey lay her head?

FOR SALE – INTERIOR WITH BODY

Under modest skirted shades
From decades ago
Light bulbs were swaying
In the draught from the hall door
Open to admit potential purchasers –
Who came to gawk in the cupboards
And sniff at the atmosphere of decay,
To view the sacred hearts and the rose-
Tangled feet of cracked arcane icons,
A gothic prayer on the wall
Festooned with a Christmas garland
And a dusty blue ribbon from an Easter
Egg on the dressing-table – careless
Of the naked body laid out on a bed,
Shy, trembling and in the way
As they passed through to the kitchen
Where laid out also on display
Were chipped cups and a little saucepan.

THE BEAUTY OF THE MOON

la beauté de la lune
Diana's lovely far from perfect face
rising from the fiery embers of her eclipse
rides west to light the fox and bear.

To praise in our dejected age
this globe that laves our night-time
dark invites derision. As if one didn't know
the features of his foolish face are but rocks
and abominable fields trampled
with man's giant steps. Yet in our *fin
de siècle* infused with green not rose
I insist I hope to always praise
la beauté de la lune.

If he what I have betrays,
when she who is not born has gone
away to a dismal State of the USA,
if my sisters grow sour
and my rival gets all the prizes,
when my share of the numerous sorrows
of the world shadows my gaze
and I am old and grey and all of that
I will exalt and love her still,
I will, I hope to always praise
the woman in the moon.

la beauté de la lune,
her heavy neck, her ragged cloud of hair
Why don't I write it plain
the beauty of the moon.